Secrets to Medicine Procurement, Health Records Management & Prescription Reading to Super Health

Wondering, HOW TO MAKE YOUR DOCTOR VISIT ROCK?

Secrets to Medicine Procurement, Health Records Management & Prescription Reading to Super Health

Wondering, HOW TO MAKE YOUR DOCTOR VISIT ROCK?

HEMANG C. PAJWANI

Worldwide Publishing by

PENDOWN PRESS

Powered by **Gullybaba Publishing House Pvt. Ltd.,**

An ISO 9001 & ISO 14001 Certified Co.,

Regd. Office: 2525/193, 1st Floor, Onkar Nagar-A, Tri Nagar, Delhi-110035

Ph.: 09350849407, 09312235086

E-mail: info@pendownpress.com

Branch Office: 1A/2A, 20, Hari Sadan, Ansari Road, Daryaganj, New Delhi–110002

Ph.: 011-45794768

Website: PendownPress.com

First Edition: 2022

ISBN: 978-93-90828-91-3

Disclaimer: This book is designed to provide information that is a guide "to make your doctor's visit rocking and make you healthy." It is sold with the understanding that the author is not engaged in rendering any professional services. Every effort has been made to make this book as complete and accurate as possible. However, there may be mistakes, both topographical and in content. Therefore, this text should be used only as a general guide and not as the ultimate source of facts about procuring medicines, maintaining Health records, and making the doctor visit successful.

Furthermore, this book contains information on facts about procuring medicines, maintaining health records, and making the doctor visit successful, that is currently only up to the printing date. The purpose of this book is to educate and entertain. The author shall have neither liability nor responsibility to any person or entity with respect to any loss or damage caused or alleged to have been caused, directly or indirectly, by the information contained in this book.

Layout and Cover Designed by Pendown Graphics Team

DEDICATION

I dedicate this book to all patients and their family members to make Doctor's visits rocking and keep you healthy.

CONTENTS

Introduction

How can you be a real life hero?

Contrary to popular belief, you need not be a Spiderman or Shaktiman, nor do you need to wear a cap, or even be a politician. Simply put, if your acts are heroic, you will emerge as a hero for sure.

1. **Let go of the ego of yours:** The first and foremost thing that you should do is to let off your ego. You should not attach a certain price to yourself. Make yourself available for the right cause and right people, without attaching a Self Tag.
2. **Initiate the particular shift you wish to determine:** Thought without action is like abortion. If you are determined for something, say plantation drive in your area, some economic activities that will provide mass employment, some move for the environment, etc., do not move about the right moment or something called "favourable condition."
3. **Take responsibility for your failure and give credit to someone else for the success:** Initiate something big that will create a big impact on the people around you. Pursue your plan consistently, learn how to take optimum use of the people

around you, try to achieve the desired outcome in a specified amount of time. If the plan turns out to be a fiasco, come forward, take the responsibility (of your failure). But, when your plan becomes successful, take credit to someone else in your group.

4. **Be prepared to act when others are actually passive:** Do not act like average. Be the front runner. When you believe in something, stick to it. Do not let your determination die down, simply because most of the people are opposing it. If you can clearly see you goal, rest assured, you will achieve it. Mind, at the initial phases, you will find most of the people talking exactly the opposite. But, as you refuse to budge, and keep on doing the things, uninterruptedly, you will achieve both—the target as well as the confidence of the people.
5. **Perform arbitrary actions associated with kindness:** The act of kindness is independent of an auspicious moment. If you see politicians' kindness related actions at the time of election, or a famous person in your area distributing clothes on his or her birthday, do not get the impression (wrong) that kindness' actions are occasion-bound. Just start doing acts of kindness. Arrange tuition fees for a poor student, buy a noon-time meal for your needy rather than offering income, take an aged neighbor to a healthcare appointment, donate blood/platelets.

6. **Do not Advertise your Accomplishments:** You may find it paradoxical, but it is irrefutably true. You need not do anything for your society with a motive. You should not think like "As I want to be a hero, I must give charity, actions related to kindness and advertise every feet of accomplishment." Instead, think like "I am committed to the welfare of my people. I will keep on doing good things, irrespective of what people think about me. For me, kindness is not an investment. It is true." If you evolve your mind and become altruist by nature, rest assure, you will emerge as a hero.
7. **Donate Blood/Platelets:** Educate people about how their blood/platelets can help save lives. Set an example of your own. Donate blood. Educate near and dear one about the fundamentals of healthcare and stand beside them whenever they are in need.

ACKNOWLEDGEMENT

I am grateful to My father, Late Mr. Chandrakant Pajwani, My mother, Late Mrs. Pravina Pajwani and all family members and friends who always supported me and nurtured me.

Knowledge Byte 1

Doctor's Visit & Second Opinion

Topics to be covered:

1. 5 Things You Should NOT Do Before A Doctor's Appointment
2. Steps to make Doctor's visit successful
3. When and how to go for Second opinion
4. How to Read and understand prescription

5 Things You Should NOT Do Before A Doctor's Appointment:

1. Do not drink coffee before a blood pressure test
2. Do not take medicine for cold
3. Do not get manicure or pedicure before a dermatologist appointment
4. Do not drink alcohol before a cholesterol test
5. Do not use deodorant before a mammogram

Steps to make Doctor's Visit Successful

Step 1. Booking the appointment:

1. Making your Appointment with Dr.___________
2. Call the doctor's office. Phone number:________
3. Tell the receptionist on the phone you are a new/old patient to see Dr.______________________
4. Tell him/her you have trouble waiting and would like the first appointment of the day or the first appointment after lunch.
5. Make an appointment.
6. Ask the receptionist if you can visit the clinic before your appointment to see the clinic and take any necessary paperwork home to fill it out.

   Optional: Leaving a Message (If your call to the doctor's office goes to voicemail, leave a message.)

   a. Say your full name.
   b. Say you were looking to make an appointment with Dr.______________
   c. Say why you wanted to make an appointment (checkup, you're not feeling well, etc.)
   d. Say your phone number slowly.
   e. Hang up the phone.

Step 2. Before you leave for the Appointment, Make sure you have:

1. Insurance Card.
2. Write down the symptoms you visit the doctor.
3. Your family medical history.

4. A list of Health goals and concerns to discuss with your Healthcare Provider.
5. A notebook for taking notes during the visit.
6. Your complete health records.
7. Packages/bottles/strips of medication you are taking.
8. Reason of the current medication you are taking.
9. List of allergies.
10. Your calendar, in case you need to schedule other doctor appointments or test.
11. Your health supporter, a person you trust to go with your doctor.

Step 3. Entering the Doctor's Office:

1. Walk up to the receptionist.
2. Tell them your name, your doctor's name, and the time of your appointment.

Step 4. Inform the doctor:

1. List the primary problem/concern
2. When did the symptoms begin?
3. Have you experienced these symptoms before? If so, when and what was the treatment?
4. Updates to your medical history (i.e. has anything in your medical history changed since you last saw this doctor?)
5. Recent lifestyle changes (i.e. stress, personal issues, sudden weight loss or gain)

Step 5. Questions to ask the doctor:

1. Ask the doctor to explain the diagnosis and what caused the illness?
2. What are my treatment options?
3. Do I need to modify my behavior? If so, how?
4. Could the medicines I'm taking be causing my symptoms?
5. Do I have any other conditions that could be causing my symptoms or making them worse?
6. How will I know the medications are working?
7. What are the risks and benefits and possible side effects?
8. Is there anything else I should know?
9. How much of each medication should be taken and how often?
10. Should the medication be taken with food or drink?
11. What are foods or activities to avoid while taking the medication?
12. Is it OK to take the medication with other medications the person is taking?
13. What is the test and why is it needed?
14. Is there anything the person needs to do to prepare for the test?
15. When will we know the results?
16. When should I come back for another visit?
17. Will you refer me to a specialist?
18. If a doctor makes a referral to someone else: ask "How do I make the appointment?"

Step 5. Before living the doctor's chamber:

1. Are there more things to do that will help the person feel better?
2. How soon should the person feel better?
3. What should I do if they don't feel better?
4. Are there warning signs I should look for? What do I do if I see them?
5. Make sure all questions that you and the individual have are answered.
6. Write down - Additional Notes:

Step 6. After the Appointment - Back at Home:

1. Ask your family members to talk to you about how your appointment went.
2. Write down anything that you would do differently for your next appointment.
3. Show your family members any paperwork from the doctor's office.
4. Make any future appointments for lab tests, x-rays, or visits to other doctors.
5. Check the prescription and order the medicines as required.
6. Whenever medicines arrive check invoice, medicines and keep in the storage as mentioned on the medicines. Do not forget to keep the medicines away from the reach of children.
7. If possible. Please write down the dose to be taken on a pack of medicines.

8. Whichever medicines are not useful or discontinued, keep a side and store at the different place. Ask your local pharmacist to dispose of it.
9. Call the doctor back if the person does not get better or if their symptoms worsen.

When to go for a second opinion by patients?

People make mistakes every day, and doctors are not immune to this fact. What's more, some doctors are more conservative while others tend to be more aggressive. So their findings and recommendations can vary dramatically. For this reason, more and more patients are getting second opinions after a diagnosis. Whether your doctor recommends surgery, makes a cancer diagnosis or identifies a rare disease, there are many benefits to getting a second opinion. These benefits include everything from the peace of mind and confirmation to a new diagnosis or a different treatment plan.

Even if your second opinion just confirms what you already know, it can still be beneficial. Afterward, you will know that you have done everything you can to ensure that you have the correct diagnosis and a treatment plan that feels right to you. A second opinion can also offer insight into additional treatment options that the first doctor may not have mentioned. As a result, you become more informed about what is available to you and can make an educated decision about your health care and your treatment plan.

Top 5 Reasons to Get a Second Opinion

While you do not need a reason to get a second opinion, there are times when getting a second opinion may be the best course of action. What's more, if the two doctors you see vastly disagree, then it might be wise to get a third opinion. Keep in mind, too, that the second opinion is not necessarily the right opinion. The key is to keep digging until the diagnosis and treatment make sense to you:

1. Get a second opinion if you have undergone treatment but your symptoms continue. No one knows your body better than you do. And if your symptoms persist even after treatment, it may be time to seek the advice of different doctors and specialists. Too often, people do not advocate for themselves. Instead, they assume that they will always have to live with chronic pain or uncomfortable feelings. But remember, the only way you are going to get the treatment that works is if you get the right diagnosis. So if you are not feeling better and your symptoms are not going away, do not settle for that. Reach out to other doctors for their opinions.
2. Get a second opinion if you are diagnosed with a rare disease. Sometimes diseases are so rare that there is very little research behind them. When this happens, it can be frustrating and frightening to discover you have been diagnosed with something so rare. But you are not alone. What's more, there are nearly 7,000 known rare disorders with more discovered each year according to the Genetic and Rare Diseases Information Center. Because there is so little information available regarding rare diseases and disorders, it is

important to do your research, because the risk of misdiagnosis is significant. Look for doctors and specialists who have treated your disorder and get their opinion. This will help ensure that you are getting the best treatment possible for your condition.

3. Get a second opinion if the recommended treatment is risky, involves surgery, is invasive or has lifelong consequences. It is never wise to agree to surgery or another invasive procedure without exploring your options. Yet, some people feel that if a doctor suggests a procedure, they have to agree to it. But remember it is your body and your life. You absolutely have a say in what treatments you agree to. As a result, it may be wise to get a second opinion if your doctor is recommending something as serious as surgery. Being proactive and gathering more information will give you a greater degree of control over your treatment in the end.
4. Get a second opinion if you are diagnosed with cancer. With something as serious as cancer, having the input from another expert simply makes sense. Not only can a cancer diagnosis be confusing and overwhelming, but it also is a life-changing event. Therefore, it is important to be as informed as possible about your prognosis and the possible treatment options available to you. Keep in mind that no one doctor is completely informed about the findings from every single study and clinical trial in the country. Doctors are

only human. That's why you need to advocate for yourself. Getting additional opinions just improves the likelihood that you will walk away with the best treatment plan possible. What's more, some health insurance providers require a second opinion when it comes to a cancer diagnosis.

5. Get a second opinion if your gut reaction tells you something is off. By all means, if you are not comfortable with the diagnosis or the recommended treatment, get a second opinion. You should never agree to a procedure or treatment plan when you don't feel good about it. Trust your gut and gather more information. Ask questions about your prescriptions. Talk to friends. Meet with a new doctor. And read about your condition. No one should ever feel like they have to follow the doctor's orders without asking questions and gathering more information. Very few health care decisions have to be made on the spot. So if something doesn't feel right, then, by all means, research your situation and talk with another doctor.

How to Request a Second Opinion

There are several different ways you can start the conversation about a second opinion with your doctor, including:

1. Telling your doctor you want to be sure that you explore all your treatment options, so you'd like to get the opinion of a non-surgical specialist in the case of a recommendation for surgery or of

other types of oncologists (medical, radiation, and surgical) if you're diagnosed with cancer, for example.

2. Letting your doctor know that you always talk to more than one expert when you need to make an important decision, whether that's a medical, financial, or personal decision.
3. Asking your doctor if he or she were diagnosed with your condition, what doctor's opinion would they seek.
4. Letting your doctor know that you'd like the opinion of a physician that specializes in treating your condition.
5. Telling your doctor that a medical second opinion would give you peace of mind that your diagnosis and treatment plan are the best option for you.

Even if your second opinion doesn't change your diagnosis or treatment plan, you can move forward with peace of mind of knowing you've gathered the information you need to make an informed decision about your care.

P.S. – Remember, you are not being difficult nor are you in denial about your situation when you ask for a second opinion. You are being smart and empowered. You should always take an active part in your health care, and getting a second opinion is an important part of that process. What's more, most doctors expect and encourage second opinions. So, be upfront with your physician about your desire to gather more information. And if he doesn't support you or gives you a difficult time, it might be time for a new doctor.

P.S.S. – Even if your second opinion doesn't change your diagnosis or treatment plan, you can move forward with peace of mind of knowing you've gathered the information you need to make an informed decision about your care.

Knowledge Byte 2

Prescriptions – Ideal Prescription

A prescription, often abbreviated x or Rx, is a health care program implemented by a physician or other qualified health care practitioner in the form of instructions that govern the plan of care for an individual patient. The term often refers to a health care provider's written authorization for a patient to purchase a prescription drug from a pharmacist.

When you get a new prescription from your doctor, you may not be able to decode what is written on it. Many people blame this on the fact that physicians are notorious for poor handwriting. In most cases, however, you wouldn't be able to read it anyway because doctors use Latin abbreviations and medical terminology on prescriptions that are not decipherable by the general public. This can make reading a prescription very difficult, but it isn't impossible.

Method 1. Decoding the Prescription yourself.

Step 1. Know the parts of the prescription.

There are certain pieces of information that your doctor will always include on a prescription. The doctor's professional information, such as his/her name, address, and phone number, will be at the top of the form. In the upper section of the prescription sheet, there will be a place for your name, your age or birth date, your address, and the date the prescription is given to you.

This will include the medicine she is prescribing, the dosage, how many pills to take per dose, and how each dose should be taken.

There will also be information for the pharmacist about how much of the medicine to give you when you fill it the first time and how many times you can refill it.

Your doctor will also sign and date the bottom to verify that it was prescribed by a professional.

If the prescription is for a controlled substance – one that the government has decided has the potential for "abuse or dependence," such as morphine or methadone – certain additional requirements must be included. The form must stipulate the number of refills (if any) and must be written in ink or typewritten. It must be manually signed by the prescribing physician.

The prescription form will vary depending on what your doctor uses. For example, there may be boxes that she fills in for a number of refills or it may be generated by a computer. Regardless of how it is written, the same basic information must always be written on the prescription form.

Many practitioners will now send prescriptions electronically to your Electronic Health record storage service providers of your choice. This is considered easier and more convenient by many practitioners, and also it helps to systematize your health records at one place.

Step 2. Understand how to read the drug name.

The main purpose of your prescription is to let the pharmacist know what drug you need in what concentration. Don't worry if you don't recognize the name of the drug. Typically, your doctor will write out the generic name for the drug. This is because the brand names for drugs can be spelled similarly and it might cause confusion or error at the pharmacy.

If your doctor wants you to take a particular brand of medicine, she can write a note to your pharmacist that indicates this need. It will say something along the lines of "no substitution" or "brand name medically necessary."

There might also be a box on the prescription somewhere that indicates if your doctor prefers the generic or brand name version of the medication.

Step 3. Read the dosage information correctly.

The number behind the name of the drug is the amount you should take per dose. It will vary depending on the type of medication that you are taking. For example, most pills will be in milligrams, but measurements can also appear in grams or micrograms. The doctor may write out the full word for this or she may write the abbreviations. The abbreviation for milligrams is mg, g is for grams, and mcg is for micrograms.

If you are taking a liquid medicine or medicine by syringe, the dosage information will be in millilitres. The abbreviation for this is ml.

Step 4. Learn the abbreviations for dosage methods (for details visit annexure).

On your prescription, the line underneath the drug and dosage concentration will be the instructions on how many doses you should take at one time and the method that should be used to take the medication. The main problem with being able to read these is that typically, doctors use medical shorthand, some based on Latin phrases, that you are not able to understand unless you have a medical background.

For the number of doses to take at one time, the doctor might write an i for the number of doses you need to take at a time. For example, if you are supposed to take 3 pills per dose, your doctor might write iii on your prescription. She may also write sig, which means to take it as it is labeled to be taken. There are other doctors, however, who will just write what you are supposed to have, such as "1 tab," which indicates how much you should take.

After the amount per day, the doctor will write how to administer your medication. Each method has an abbreviation that is Latin based. Po means to take it orally, pr means per rectum or suppository, sl means sublingual or under the tongue, IV means injected into the vein, IM means injected into the muscle, and SQ means subcutaneous or under the skin.

Step 5. Decode how you should take the medication.
Next to the dosage methods, the doctor will write an abbreviation for how often you should take your medication. This describes the number of times a day or week you should take your medication. Next to this, she will write any special circumstances under which you should take the medication. This will indicate things such as the need to take the medication with food.

The description of how often you should take your medicine is abbreviated using Latin phrases just like the method. Qd means every day, od means once daily, bid means twice a day, tid means three times a day, and qid means four times a day. The abbreviation qam means every morning, qpm means every night, q2h means every 2 hours, qod means every other day, and hs means at bedtime.

Any special instructions are also abbreviated based on Latin phrases. Pc means after meals or not on an empty stomach, ac means before meals, qhs means each night, and prn means as needed.

Some doctors will write how often it should be taken instead, such as writing "daily" next to the dosage information. For controlled substances such as pain killers, she may write out the reason for taking the medication, such as the phrase "pain" if you need certain medications after surgery or for a chronic condition.

Step 6. Look for refills.
Your doctor may authorize a certain number of refills for your prescription without needing you to come in for another examination or follow-up.

Method 2. Asking Questions to Experts

Step 1. Write out your questions.

Before you go to the doctor, you should have some questions ready in case you get prescribed medication. You should ask about the medication you are taking and all the details involved in its administration. This includes questions about the name of the medication, how often you are supposed to take it, the manner in which to take it, what disease the medication is treating, and if there are any side effects you should expect to have. You can also ask about what to do if you miss a dose and when you should stop taking the medication. It's a good idea to write these out in advance so you don't forget them.

You might also want to ask what taking the medicine will accomplish, if there is a less expensive alternative, or if there are any interactions with other prescribed or over the counter medications, dietary supplements, foods, or herbal supplements.

Step 2. Ask for an explanation of the prescription.

When you visit your doctor, if you are not exactly sure how to read the prescription you are given, you can ask them to explain their instructions for the medication before you leave the office. Use the questions you prepared before you went to the office to understand more about your prescription. Make sure you fully understand any terms they use or any descriptions that you may not know the meaning of.

Make sure you write down the answers that give you so you will be able to compare this with what you get from the pharmacy. This way you make sure you are always taking the right medication in the right doses.

Step 3. Request that the pharmacist review the prescription.

One way to make sure that all the right procedures are followed in regards to your prescription is to have your pharmacist review it when you drop it off and when you pick it up. Mistakes can take place when a pharmacist reads the directions differently than what the doctor intended.

You can help prevent dangerous medication errors by double checking and asking the pharmacist to verify the prescription with your physician.

If you have any questions about the prescription or the medication, ask your pharmacist.

Step 4. Review the information your pharmacist gives you.

Once you get your prescription filled, you will get a pamphlet from the pharmacist that explains the medication you are taking, what side effects may occur, and many other medicine intricacies that you may have questions about it. The pharmacist will usually offer to explain the medication and answer any lingering questions you have about your medications.

If you experience side effects or interaction effects, you should call your healthcare provider immediately to report them and ask for a confirmation of your intended prescription, as well as further instructions for taking the medication.

Knowledge Byte 3

Maintaining Health Records

An accurate written record detailing all aspects of patient monitoring is important, not only because it forms an integral part of the provision of care or nursing management of the patient, but because it also contributes to the circulation of information amongst the different teams involved in the patient's treatment or care.

In a legal sense, documentation and record keeping is also there for the protection of the nurse or healthcare professional.

A well-kept record can protect the practitioner in instances where the legal defence of their actions is required. Documentation also ensures a matter of professionalisation and proof of the improvement of practices.

Types of Record-Keeping Used in Healthcare:

- Hand-written records
- Computer-based systems (electronic)
- Some organisations or employers will use a combination of both.

You'll be expected to be able to comply with whatever requirements your employer or organisation sets for record-keeping. That means you'll need to:

- Ensure that you are up to date on the information systems and tools in your workplace including their security, confidentiality and appropriate usage;
- Protect any passwords or details given to you to enable your access to any systems;
- Make sure written records are not left in public places where unauthorised people might see them (including any electronic systems or displays);
- Ensure that an entry is made in the patient's medical record whenever a health professional sees a patient.

Components of a patient's records include:

1. Medical records
2. Nursing records/progress notes
3. Medication charts
4. Laboratory orders and reports
5. Vital signs observation charts
6. Handover sheets and admission
7. Discharge and transfer checklists/ letters
8. Patient's assessment forms, such as nutrition or pressure area care assessment.

Principles of Good Record Keeping

Some key factors underpin good record keeping. The patient's records should:

1. Be factual, consistent and accurate;
2. Be updated as soon as possible after any recordable event;
3. Provide current information on the care and condition of the patient;
4. Be documented clearly in such a way that the text cannot be erased;
5. Be consecutive and accurately dated, timed and all entries signed (including any alterations);
6. All original entries should be legible. Draw a clear line through any changes and sign and date;
7. Not include abbreviations, slang or jargon as not all workplaces or organisations will use the same terminology;
8. Records must be stored securely and should only be destroyed following your local policy;
9. Avoid meaningless phrases, speculation and offensive subjective statements/insulting or derogatory language;
10. Identify the patient by recording patient's name, date of birth and hospital number on each page of the record (three approved identifiers) or follow your local policies on how to identify patient's records;
11. Still be legible if photocopied or scanned.

Common Deficiencies in Record Keeping.

Poor record keeping hampers the care that patients receive and makes it difficult for healthcare professionals to defend their practice.

The most common deficiencies in record keeping include:

- An absence of clarity
- Inaccuracies
- Spelling mistakes
- Missing information
- Failure to record action taken when a problem has been identified.

Benefits of Good Record Keeping

Record keeping is a tool for professional practice and one that should help the care process. It is not separate and not an optional extra to be fitted in if circumstances allow.

A record should be made as soon as possible after the patient is seen or the procedure is complete. It's important that accurate records are made in the patient's notes and should include interventions and any response to the interventions.

The importance of good record keeping are:

- Record keeping makes the continuity of care easier;
- Record keeping promotes better communication and dissemination of information between members of the multi-professional team;

- Helps to address complaints or legal processes;
- Supports clinical audit, research, allocation of resources and performance planning;
- Helps to identify risks and enables the early detection of complications;
- Supports patient care and patient-centred communication;
- Supports effective clinical judgement;
- Supports delivery of services;
- Helps improve accountability;
- Shows how decisions were made relating to the patient's care.

Legal Issues in Record Keeping

The patient's records are occasionally required as evidence before a court of law, or to investigate a complaint at a local, organisation level.

Sometimes records may be requested by professional governing bodies when investigating claims related to misconduct (NMC 2010).

Therefore, you must take care about what you write. Not only will you be asked to formally explain your records in the event of, for instance, a complaint from a patient/client, but registered nurses have both a professional and legal duty of care.

It is therefore critical to keep up-to-date with the legal requirements and best practices of record-keeping, proving that:

A comprehensive nursing assessment of the patient has been undertaken including care that has been provided and planned;

Relevant information is included together with any actions that have been taken in response to changes in patients' conditions;

The duty of care to the patient has been provided and that no acts or omissions have compromised a patient's safety;

Arrangements have been made for the ongoing care of the patient.

Paper Medical Records Definition

Medical records are a combination of self-reported patient information and clinical diagnostic notes traditionally stored on paper-based mediums.

Advantages of Paper Medical Records:

1. **Reduced Upfront Costs:** With paper medical records, all you need to get started is paper, files, and a locked cabinet to store all the documents. That's not going to set you back nearly as much as a high-end electronic health record (EHR) system which requires cloud servers and other fancy tech.

   At the same time, you don't need extensive training programs to upskill nurses and doctors on the intricacies of managing electronic health systems. These costs are incurred during implementation of an EHR, and during onboarding a new healthcare provider.

2. **Ease of Use in a Familiar Format:** There's a reason why paper medical records were an industry mainstay for several decades. It's easy to pull up information from a file, examine previous notes and medical charts, and record new observations.

   If the information is written clearly, there can be fewer complications to reading charts and notes on paper. Software means you have to enter the correct keywords and user IDs to access data. Not everyone is tech-savvy and able to transition to a new technology.

3. **Physical Form Factor:** Electronic medical records sound great on paper (no pun intended) but what do you do when there's an emergency?

   When time is of the essence, such as multiple trauma victims requiring immediate action, slow loading times and unfamiliar interfaces may waste precious minutes as nurses search databases using keywords and scroll past various screens to access prior records.

   Paper records are advantageous in this sense: a physical file with all previous charts and medical history neatly sorted in one place. Plus, the data can be physically passed around from one person to another seamlessly. Of course, all of this depends on the previous notes being neatly written, properly organized, and readily accessible.

4. **Easier to Customize:** Another advantage of paper medical records is that the form is customizable to the requirements of each hospital/doctor without

the need for any technical overhaul. Need a new template? Just design one on a standard text editor and you're good to go.

With electronic health records, however, you'll need a software developer to make adjustments to the code and back end systems. That's both time consuming and costly.

There are some problems with paper medical records:

1. **Storage Isn't Scalable:** Unlike electronic medical records stored on cloud servers, paper medical records need physical space for storage purposes.

   A single cloud server could store hundreds of thousands of patient medical records, but physical files to cater to that capacity require a lot of space. And it's not just a matter of assigning an empty room and stuffing files there — these are valuable repositories of data and require careful handling. Hence, you probably need temperature-controlled rooms and other mechanisms to ensure data integrity.

2. **Lack of Backups & Limited Security:** What do you do if there's a fire that wipes out all your physical files? Or a moth infestation that, quite literally, eats up all your data? Physical files, once lost, are impossible to recover. Electronic records, however, have data backup and storage, so even if a malicious entity manages to infiltrate and get access, there's still a fallback option.

3. **Time Consuming & Error Prone:** Paper medical records mean you need a manual written process which is both time consuming and comes with a higher degree of error. If you've ever attempted to read a doctor's notes, you'll know that the writing isn't always legible and therefore can be hard to interpret.

   An electronic system doesn't have these problems—records aren't handwritten, so the legibility issue isn't an issue at all. Plus you don't have to search for patient files in a physical cabinet— the software does that for you (instantly).

4. **Inconsistent Layouts:** While paper based records can be easier to customize, it also means that the layout and format of information can be inconsistent from one record to the next. Electronic records have a consistent format which healthcare providers can get accustomed to.

   When paper based records have different layouts, it extends the time needed to get the (potentially life saving) information needed for a patient. Healthcare providers can get familiar with a few formats of data, and this reduces the time needed to find and analyze information.

5. **No Clear Audit Trails & Version History:** Paper records don't have built-in version histories and audit trails. Knowing who made which edits and additions requires that the physician signs the records each time. If changes are made, it's not easy to locate where the changes were and who made them.

This is important when auditing records or trying to find a previous physician who added information. An element of human error is always possible. Electronic health records have logs and version records that simplify auditing and tracking by automating it.

Paper Vs. Electronic Medical Record Keeping

When it comes to deciding between paper vs. electronic records, there are a few things you must take into consideration.

Electronic health records are far more secure than paper records as they're not at risk during a catastrophic event.

It's also easier to retain accountability in electronic health records—each entry log is consistent with a specific individual. This factor makes it easier to keep track of who is diagnosing patients and recommending medical outcomes.

Lastly, EHRs ship in a customized format that helps with things like legibility and accuracy of medical data. Paper-based records can involve human error and a loss of data integrity.

EMR Vs. EHR – What is the Difference?

Electronic medical records (EMRs) are a digital version of the paper charts in the clinician's office. An EMR contains the medical and treatment history of the patients in one practice. EMRs have advantages over paper records. For example, EMRs allow clinicians to:

Track data over time

Easily identify which patients are due for preventive screenings or checkups

Check how their patients are doing on certain parameters—such as blood pressure readings or vaccinations.

Monitor and improve overall quality of care within the practice.

But the information in EMRs doesn't travel easily out of the practice. In fact, the patient's record might even have to be printed out and delivered by mail to specialists and other members of the care team. In that regard, EMRs are not much better than a paper record.

Electronic health records (EHRs) do all those things—and more. EHRs focus on the total health of the patient—going beyond standard clinical data collected in the provider's office and inclusive of a broader view on a patient's care. EHRs are designed to reach out beyond the health organization that originally collects and compiles the information. They are built to share information with other health care providers, such as laboratories and specialists, so they contain information from all the clinicians involved in the patient's care. The National Alliance for Health Information Technology stated that EHR data "can be created, managed, and consulted by authorized clinicians and staff across more than one healthcare organization."

The information moves with the patient—to the specialist, the hospital, the nursing home, the next state or even across the country. In comparing the differences between record types, HIMSS Analytics stated that, "The EHR represents the ability to easily share medical information among stakeholders and to have a patient's information follow him or her through the various modalities of care engaged by that individual." EHRs are designed to be accessed by all people involved in the patient's care—including the patients themselves. Indeed, that is an explicit expectation in the Stage 1 definition of "meaningful use" of EHRs.

And that makes all the difference. Because when information is shared in a secure way, it becomes more powerful. Health care is a team effort, and shared information supports that effort. After all, much of the value derived from the health care delivery system results from the effective communication of information from one party to another and, ultimately, the ability of multiple parties to engage in interactive communication of information.

Benefits of EHRs

With fully functional EHRs, all members of the team have ready access to the latest information allowing for more coordinated, patient-centered care. With EHRs:

The information gathered by the primary care provider tells the emergency department clinician about the patient's life threatening allergy, so that care can be adjusted appropriately, even if the patient is unconscious.

A patient can log on to his own record and see the trend of the lab results over the last year, which can help motivate him to take his medications and keep up with the lifestyle changes that have improved the numbers.

The lab results run last week are already in the record to tell the specialist what she needs to know without running duplicate tests.

The clinician's notes from the patient's hospital stay can help inform the discharge instructions and follow-up care and enable the patient to move from one care setting to another more smoothly.

So, yes, the difference between "electronic medical records" and "electronic health records" is just one word. But in that word there is a world of difference.

Disadvantage of EHR

3 Steps to Maintain Your Personal Electronic Health Records.

How do you usually maintain your health records? We bet, you maintain a file of all the prescriptions, scans and tests, health screening reports, discharge summaries, and store it in a safe place.

However, there are several problems associated with maintaining physical health records:

One problem is that you must be extremely organized in order to make sure that you keep the records in the same file in the same location every time you take it out. If not, they can never be found when you need them the most!

Another problem is that paper can deteriorate over the years. You may even end up losing an important record and this may prove costly to you.

Carrying physical records with you every time you travel can prove to be extremely cumbersome!

Now, it is much simpler to maintain all your health records in one place and never lose them again. Moreover, you have easier access to medical records anytime and from any place you want!

How can you go for Electronic Health Records?

Simply, get registered with Electronic Health Records service providers.

Before registering with any Electronic Health Record service, please check the feature or benefits, it should have. You have complete health records, even when you have submitted all the original documents at the time insurance claim.

Benefits/Features List which should have in your Electronic Health Record service Providers.

- **Pocket-sized Lifesaving Identity Card–** Health records are available even when you do not have mobile.
- **Lifesaving Corporate Identity card–** it provides benefits of Electronic Health Records and Corporate identity card.
- **It should be Cloud based–** Health records are available 24/7.
- **Works on all platforms–** Stay connected from anywhere. No need to buy special device.
- **Simple Interface–** No need to be tech-savvy.
- **Completely secured–** it should have minimum 256 Bits data security (Equivalent to Bank transaction)
- **Health History brief on your health card–** By viewing your health card, anyone could able to see your Name, Address, Age, emergency contact details, blood group, Mini Health History (allergies, blood pressure, diabetes...), Health Insurance policy name and number, etc.

- **Self-manageable Health card–** No need to approach the customer service team to update your Health History.
- **Health records should be easily accessible by Healthcare Providers with complete privacy–** In case of emergency Health records are vital and it's good to treat in a better way. It should have complete control in your hand to whom to share your Electronic Health Records.

Conclusion

Digital Health records, in contrast to paper-based Health Records, are health records in which data are accessible to patients and not just providers. Digital Health Records provide more benefits to patients than paper-based, as increasing and widespread Internet access and mobile device use allow patients to access health information via the Internet or telecommunication devices, such as mobile phones, personal digital assistants, and tablet computers.

Digital Health Records have the potential to help patients and providers identify medical conditions and prescriptions from numerous locations, which may minimize medical errors and identify improvements to health behaviours during emergencies, when patients present to a new provider, or paper-based records are not accessible.

Knowledge Byte 4

Procuring & Consuming The Medicines

How To Procure Medicine?

A visit to the pharmacy or filling out your prescription online can be mundane tasks you perform regularly, but you can still make your purchase more effective bearing a few things in mind:

Carry the prescription

Why? You know your dad's medicines, you've been buying them for years. Your memory may serve you best, but the pharmacist can serve you better with a prescription in hand – ensuring you don't absent-mindedly walk away with the wrong dose or the wrong quantity.

Insist on a bill or a receipt

Ask for a bill once you're done, no matter how familiar you are with the store! A bill or receipt offers some degree of accountability for the goods sold. Additionally, if your health insurance plan includes a domiciliary cover, you will need the receipts for reimbursement.

Understand what an active-ingredient is

While the same active ingredient could be present in drugs marketed by different manufacturers, the inherent purpose and use of the drug remains the same. The same active ingredient may have a slightly different colour, formulation, taste or packaging with a different manufacturer. When in doubt, always reach out to your physician, another good use of carrying a prescription with the doctor's contact information on it.

Look out for the expiration date as well as date of manufacture

In a hurry to spot the expiration date, we often overlook the obvious– the date of manufacture. A product that expires within a month could have been manufactured two-five years ago. Given climatic conditions or storage conditions, there's every possibility the drug is not safe to consume closer to its expiry.

Don't miss out on special discounts and services

Pharmacies are pretty much like any retail outlet in ensuring a good experience for customers while shopping with them. You may have noticed the offers and conveniences added at most pharmacies or while ordering medicines online. These special services include discounts or loyalty programs for customers, free home delivery, and alternative payment options through leading payment gateways. Make sure you are not missing out on these options!

Essential Tips and Tricks to consider before making a purchase from an Online Pharmacy

- **Look for Pharmacies that Require a Valid Prescription–** This is very important to consider before purchasing medicines online. Pharmacies that need a prescription are most likely to sell quality and genuine medicines. If you come across advertisements or promotions where you can purchase medicines without a prescription, then it's a Red Flag. By providing a Prescription, you can also make sure that you get the right drug and in the right dosage.

  A prescription needs to be valid and it indicates that a medical practitioner has approved of the drug you are about to consume. This is the only correct way to go about.

- **Online Pharmacy Should be Licensed–** Make sure to check the quality of the online pharmacy you are purchasing from. The Pharmacy should be licensed to sell drugs and deliver them in the state that you live in. For example, Apollo Pharmacy is accredited with International Quality Certification. This certification guarantees the quality of the drugs being sold.

- **Avoid Purchasing Drugs from Foreign Websites–** It is essential that you avoid the purchase of drugs from Websites which aren't from your country. This causes delivery problems; drug information and dosage vary from place to place. Stick to the Country you are in and it is recommended to purchase from the same trusted pharmacy every time.

- **Never Purchase Medicines You aren't sure of!–** Purchasing medicines that you aren't sure of causes potential risks of health complications through drug interference. OTC Drugs are serious drugs and not to be taken lightly while consuming.
- **Pharmacies Need to Answer Your Questions–** Always look for Online Pharmacies which provide pharmacists who clear all your doubts and answer your questions. Make sure your Pharmacy grants access to qualified pharmacists and shoot out any question which is on your mind.
- **Beware of Shady Websites Trying to Convince You With Offers–** The Drug quality should be of your primary importance. Don't get chicaned for offers and make sure that you trust the pharmacy or vendor selling the medicines.
- **Prioritize Pharmacies With Good Customer Supports–** Any good Pharmacy will be ready to assist you even post the purchase. Make sure you opt for these Pharmacies as they will also have good replacement options.
- **Watch out for the Expiry Date of the Drug–** The Expiry Date of the Drug is very important and a lot of good online stores will generally mention the complete details. Make sure that you buy the most recently manufactured medicine. A lot of medicines are outdated due to the research on advanced Human Care.

- **Avoid Shopping Overseas**– One reason why gangs and criminals tend to include shipping in their schemes is that it's really hard for law enforcement to search for contraband with any thoroughness without slowing down commerce and hurting business. Simply put, there is just so much being shipped across the planet that the cops can't search it all. That means there is greater space for bad actors to hawk their wares abroad. Further, the infinity of the Internet is nearly impossible to scour of criminals. Putting the two together—ordering medication online from an over-the-seas pharmacy—opens up all kinds of risk.

General precautions

There are a few other things to always keep in mind, like:

- Never accept medication where the packaging seems damaged or puffed up
- Never accept medicines that don't look authentic or if they look tampered with
- Avoid self-medication
- Check dosage
- Do not reuse the prescription.
- Do not share the prescription with anyone having similar problems.
- Check expiry dates.
- Check the concentration of medicines prescribed, 200mg, 25mg etc.

- If the prescribed medicine is not available, request your doctor to prescribe a substitute, do not ask the pharmacist to give any other similar medicines.
- Do not buy OTC medicines by asking friends, relatives or pharmacy shop salesmen.

Steps to identify fake drugs:

- Check the physical appearance of the medicine (color, texture, shape, and packaging)
- Check to see if it smells and tastes the same when you use it.
- Alert your pharmacist or your doctor if you have any doubt on counterfeiting (packaging defect, side effect...)
- A very low drug price may be a warning of a fake drug; stay on your guard and compare prices.
- If you suffer any severe and/or unusual secondary effects, you may be using a counterfeit drug, talk to a doctor.

Store Medicines Safely

Where you store your medicine can affect how well it works. Learn about storing your medicine properly to keep it from getting damaged.

- Take care of your medicine.
- Know that heat, air, light, and moisture may damage your medicine.
- Store your medicines in a cool, dry place. For example, store it in your dresser drawer or a kitchen cabinet away from the stove, sink, and any

hot appliances. You can also store medicine in a storage box, on a shelf, in a closet.

- If you are like most people, you probably store your medicine in a bathroom cabinet. But the heat and moisture from your shower, bath, and sink may damage your medicine. Your medicines can become less potent, or they may go bad before the expiration date.
- Pills and capsules are easily damaged by heat and moisture. Aspirin pills break down into vinegar and salicylic acid. This irritates the stomach.
- Always keep medicine in its original container.
- Take the cotton ball out of the medicine bottle. The cotton ball pulls moisture into the bottle.
- Ask your pharmacist about any specific storage instructions.
- Keep children safe.
- Always store your medicine out of reach and out of sight of children.
- Store your medicine in a cabinet with a child latch or lock.

Do not use Damaged Medicine

- Damaged medicine may make you sick. Do not take
- Medicine that has changed color, texture, or smell, even if it has not expired
- Pills that stick together, are harder or softer than normal, or are cracked or chipped

Get rid of old Medicines

- Get rid of unused medicine safely and promptly.
- Check the expiration date on your medicine. Throw out medicines that are out of date.
- Do not keep old or unused medicine around. It goes bad and you should not use it.
- Do not flush your medicine down the toilet. This is bad for the water supply.
- To throw away medicine in the trash, first mix your medicine with something that ruins it, such as coffee grounds or kitty litter. Put the entire mixture in a sealed plastic bag.
- You can also bring unused medicines to your pharmacist.
- Use community "drug give back" programs if they are available.

Traveling With Medicine

- Do not keep medicine in the glove compartment of your car. Medicine can get too hot, cold, or wet there.
- If you are taking an airplane, keep your medicine in your carry-on luggage. To help with security at the airport:
- Keep medicine in the original bottles.
- Ask your health care provider for a copy of all your prescriptions. You may need this in case you lose, run out, or damage your medicine.

- If you have diabetes, ask your provider for a letter explaining that you have diabetes and providing a list of all your supplies. You are allowed to carry your medicine, blood glucose meter, and lancet device on a plane.

Why You Should Stop Storing Medications in the Bathroom?

Here are three very good reasons why you should never keep your medications in the bathroom.

1. Bathrooms are humid. Most pills, tablets, and capsules are designed to be taken with water - not only because water helps you wash the medication down, but also because it helps to activate the medication. Water is the first step in getting your oral medications to dissolve so the medication can work its magic in your body. Storing your medications in a humid environment makes your medications less effective by starting this process before you put the medication in your mouth.
2. High humidity can change the chemistry of your medications, often breaking them down into different substances. Ever noticed how aspirin smells like vinegar when it gets old or you leave it in the bathroom? That's because it breaks down into vinegar when exposed to humidity or it's outdated. Yuck.
3. Bathrooms get H-O-T. Unless otherwise noted, most medications should either be stored at or a few degrees below room temperature. Bathroom

heat - like hot showers or the heat from your blow dryer - can weaken medications and shorten their shelf-life.

Four simple tips for safe dosing

1. **Know the Dose:** Read all the information on the medicine label and follow the directions. Do not give a child medicine more often or in greater amounts than is stated on the package.
2. **Measure the Right Amount:** Always measure your child's dose using the dosing device (oral syringe or dosing cup) that comes with the medicine.
3. **Use the Right Tool:** If you do not have a dosing device, ask your pharmacist for one. Do not use household spoons to give medicines to children.
4. **Get Questions Answered :** If you do not understand the instructions on the label, or how to use the dosing device, talk to your pharmacist or doctor before giving the medicine.

Over-the-Counter Medicine Precautions

Know the benefits and side effects of a medicine before taking it. Use medicines only if non-drug approaches are not working.

Follow these over-the-counter medicine precautions.

- Carefully read and follow all directions on the medicine bottle and box. Or let your doctor know why you think you should take the medicine in a different way.

- Take the minimum effective dose. When using a liquid drug, use the measuring device that comes with the drug.
- Call your doctor if you think you are having a problem with your medicine. If you have been told to avoid a medicine, call your doctor before you take it.
- Do not take a medicine if you have had an allergic reaction to it in the past.
- If you are or could be pregnant, call your doctor before taking any medicine.
- Keep a list of all your medicines, including over-the-counter medicines, vitamins, and natural health products. And share the list with your doctor.

Here are some safety tips about giving children medicines.

- Do not give aspirin to anyone younger than 18 unless your doctor tells you to, because of the risk of Reye syndrome.
- Talk to your doctor before you give fever medicine to a baby who is 6 months of age or younger. This is to make sure a young baby's fever is not a sign of a serious illness. Ask your doctor what other medicines may not be safe to give your child.
- Don't take medicines in front of small children. Children are great mimics. Don't say that medicine tastes like candy.

- Keep medicines, vitamins, and natural health products tightly capped in their original containers. Store them as directed and keep them out of the reach of children.

How to remember to take medicine on time?

It's a fact - keeping up with your prescription, over-the-counter, and vitamin treatments can be a daunting task. But never fear – there are tried and true methods to help you to remember to take your daily meds on time without fail.

Here are some tips to help you remember how to take your medicine.

1. **Practice makes perfect...learn about your medicines.**

   Learning more about what your medications are used for will reinforce your adherence to your treatment plan. Learning about your medical conditions can be a strong motivator, too. This is especially important for conditions that have few, if any, symptoms to remind you it's time to take your medicine – like high blood pressure.

   Learning about side effects are important so you can recognize them if they occur. Many side effects with drug treatment are temporary, so be sure to ask your doctor about short-lived and more long-term side effects with any medication.

2. **Pill boxes.**

   Pill boxes are an organization tool for your pills that can easily be found at most pharmacies. Pill boxes have been around for a long time, and are especially useful if you easily forget if you have taken your meds each day. Pill boxes are also very useful for people who take multiple medications each day and at different times.

Older patients may especially find pill boxes convenient to use. The boxes are split into individual sections that make-up a week's worth of medicine, or more, and may even be separated by time of day. They can easily fit into travel bags or purses; however, don't leave them in a hot car.

3. **Electronic applications and pill reminders.**

Apps to help patients remember and track their medication use are convenient tools for anyone who carries a mobile phone.

For example, a pill reminder app can keep a complete list of all your medications. You could choose to get pill reminders to take your medicines at a special time, and receive prescription refill reminders right on your mobile device.

You can also add personal notes and get easy access to important information about your medicine online.

If you like visual clues, you might get a photo of your medications for easy reference on the app.

It is an easy way to have a complete list of all your medicines when you visit the doctor, dentist or other healthcare provider.

4. **Calendar alerts.**

   Maybe you prefer not to use a mobile device or just like the simple method of a calendar. Those are great tools, too. Mark your daily doses on a paper calendar at home, on your computer, or even in your little black book. Just be sure to update it frequently and mark through each dose as you take it, in case you forget from dose to dose.

   Getting into a regular routine to help you remember to take your meds is really what's most important. Find what works best for you.

5. **Tie your medication doses with a daily activity.**

   You can tie your drug doses with a daily routine like breakfast time, after a shower, or when you get ready for bed. Keep your medications in an easy-to-see (but secure) spot as a visual clue. Pretty soon taking your meds will be as routine as, well, brushing your teeth (and that might be a good time to take your meds, too).

   Be sure you keep your medications in a safe and secure area, away from curious toddlers and pets. Protect your meds from extreme heat or cold, and don't leave them in a steamy bathroom (where medicine cabinets are usually found, coincidentally). Most medications are stable at room temperature, but under extreme conditions, they can lose their potency, crumble, or even melt.

If your medicine needs to be stored in the refrigerator, consider posting a sticky note reminder on the fridge as a reminder to grab it when it's time.

If you have especially dangerous medications such as opioid painkillers, be sure to keep them safe and secure, even locked up if needed, to prevent theft or accidental ingestion by a child or pet.

6. **Get help from family members or friends:**

Many friends and family take meds, and creating a team to help remind each other to take their doses can be helpful. If you live alone, maybe a friend would text you each morning or night, when they also take their meds. If a family member you live with also takes meds, you have a built in pill reminder right there at your house. Take advantage of it.

Seniors often need help to remember their medications. If you have a loved one that takes several meds, consider helping them create a pill box, printing out pictures of their pills from the Pill ID tool, and then writing in large print what each medicine is used for, and its name and dose. Place the pictures in a conspicuous, but safe, place so that they can refer to the printouts when needed.

Large print on prescription bottles and for drug information printouts can be very helpful as older patients lose their eyesight. Your pharmacist can usually print out dosing and drug information in large type–so be sure to ask.

7. **Keep an up-to-date list of your medication names, strengths, doses, and number of remaining refills.**

   Having an easily accessible list of your medication specifics will enable you to provide this information correctly and quickly at a time when you might need it the most – in an emergency situation. Just be sure to update this information when medications are started or stopped. Remember–over-the-counter drugs, vitamins and herbal or dietary supplements count, too–so have them on your list.

   If you utilize electronic tools, you can easily update this information as needed on the free Drugs.com Medication Guide App.

8. **Ask your doctor and pharmacist to help simplify your medication regimen.**

   If all else fails, there may be ways to simplify your medication regimen to make life easier. If you take a drug two or three times per day, your doctor may be able to find a similar drug that only needs to be taken once a day.

   If you need to separate doses because you have to be careful about combining antacids or other supplements with prescription drugs due to drug interactions, your doctor may be able to find medications that do not cause an interaction.

Ask your doctor or pharmacist which medications you can safely take together at the same time to limit multiple daily doses.

Be sure to check to see if you can take your meds at breakfast, dinner, or bedtime - the most common (and often easy) times to take medications. Set up your routine around these times, if possible.

How to Take Medications Properly?

The most common way people take medications is orally (by mouth). Depending on what your doctor prescribed, your oral medication can be swallowed, chewed, or placed under your tongue to dissolve.

Medications that you swallow travel from your stomach or intestine into your bloodstream and then are carried to all parts of your body. This process is known as absorption. The speed with which absorption occurs depends on several factors:

- The type of medication you are taking (e.g., liquid or tablet)
- Whether you take your medication with food, after food or on an empty stomach
- The ability of your medication to pass into your bloodstream (Some medications have a special coating and dissolve slowly in your stomach.)
- How your medication reacts with the acid conditions in your stomach
- Whether your medication interacts with other medications you are taking at the same time
- If a quick effect is desired, your doctor may prescribe a medication that will dissolve in your mouth and rapidly enter your bloodstream.

Tablets and Capsules

In general, you should take tablets and capsules with water. Taking certain pills, such as Lipitor (atorvastatin) and Viagra (sildenafil), with grapefruit juice can cause potentially dangerous side effects. Milk can block the absorption of some antibiotics, such as Cipro (ciprofloxacin).

Your doctor or pharmacist will tell you whether to take your medication on an empty stomach or before or after eating. This information is very important because digesting food can interfere with your medication dissolving and passing into your bloodstream. Always follow the directions on your prescription.

Never break, crush, or chew any capsule or tablet unless directed to by your doctor or pharmacist. Many medications are long-acting or have a special coating and must be swallowed whole. If you have any questions about this, ask your pharmacist.

If you have trouble swallowing your medication, tell your doctor and pharmacist. They may be able to provide you with a liquid form of the medication or a pill that is smaller and easier to swallow.

Liquid Medications

Liquid medications are good for children and adults (especially older adults) who are not able to swallow tablets or capsules.

Many liquid medications, including both prescription drugs and over-the-counter drugs, are made for children and are flavored to mask the taste of the medication.

Before measuring the proper dose of liquid medication, make sure to shake the bottle as some of the medication may have "settled" at the bottom.

Most often, you'll be given medication measurements in teaspoons (remember that teaspoons are smaller than tablespoons). In medicine, a teaspoon means 5 milliliters (ml).

Your household teaspoons may hold more or less than 5 ml. Ask your pharmacist for a spoon, medicine cup, medicine dropper, or a syringe without a needle meant specifically for measuring medications. They can show you how to properly use these.

Many over-the-counter liquid medications come with a small medicine cup attached to the top of the bottle.

If the medication has been prescribed for an infant or young child, make sure to speak with your pediatrician about the proper dosage, or amount, of liquid medication for your child.

Sublingual and Buccal Medications

Certain medications are placed under the tongue (sublingual) or between the teeth and the cheek (buccal). These medications are absorbed quickly into the bloodstream through the lining of the mouth and are used to relieve symptoms almost immediately.

Some examples of sublingual medications are Nitrostat and other nitroglycerin preparations used to treat angina (chest pain) and Suboxone (buprenorphine with naloxone), which is used to treat heroin dependence and narcotic painkillers.

Other Forms of Oral Medications

Although most oral medications are swallowed, some are released in the mouth by chewing, dissolving slowly or melting on the tongue. Many of these medications are sold over-the-counter.

Chewable Tablets

Chewable tablets should be chewed until they have completely dissolved. They're not meant to be swallowed whole.

Examples of chewable tablets include Tylenol Chewable and many brands of children's vitamins.

Chewing Gum Medications

Chewing gum medications have a minimum time that they must be chewed to ensure that the entire amount of drug has been released, often up to 30 minutes.

Examples of medicated chewing gums include Nicorette Gum (nicotine) and Aspergum (aspirin).

Lozenges

Lozenges are meant to be "sucked" on like hard candy and allowed to dissolve slowly in your mouth. They should not be swallowed.

Examples of medicated lozenges include Commit (nicotine) and Cepacol (benzocaine).

Soft chew Medications

Soft chew medications are meant to melt in your mouth or to be chewed.

An example of a Soft chew medication is Rolaids Soft Chew (calcium carbonate).

Tip for Swallowing Pills

Swallowing pills can be an unpleasant and uncomfortable experience for some. If you have difficulty swallowing pills, there are things that you can do to facilitate this process.

For example, German researchers found success with the following technique called the "pop bottle method." 2 This technique was tested with tablets.

1. Open a bottle of water or soda bottle filled with water.
2. Place the tablet on your tongue and close your mouth around the opening of the bottle.
3. Tilt your head back and keep your mouth sealed around the water bottle. Don't let any air into your mouth. Suck the water into your mouth and swallow the tablet and water.

Please note that this intervention has not been tested extensively, and, if interested, you should discuss this technique with your doctor before you try it. Furthermore, if you have difficulty swallowing in general, you should probably be evaluated for dysphagia. 2

On a final note, always read the instructions carefully and take your medications as recommended. If you have any doubts or concerns, contact your doctor or pharmacist.

Branded medicine v/s Generic Medicines v/s pseudo-generic medicine.

A **branded medicine** is the original product that has been developed by a pharmaceutical company. When a company develops a new medicine, their product must undergo and pass rigorous tests and evaluations to ensure that it is both effective in curing the condition it claims to treat and safe for human use. Because pharmaceutical companies invest considerable amounts of money to develop a new medicine, they are given the sole right to manufacture and distribute the medicine for a period of time.

When a pharmaceutical company is given sole rights of manufacture and distribution, the medicine is said to have a patent on it. A patent is a technical description of what the drug is and what it is used for. For a period of time after the patent is granted, no one else can produce a drug that is the same as the patented drug; the medicine belongs exclusively to the original company. For this reason, branded medicines are the most well known and most trusted type of that particular medicine.

A **generic medicine** is a copy of the original branded product. Once the patent for the original product has run out, the pharmaceutical company who developed the medicine no longer has the exclusive right to produce and distribute the medicine. Other pharmaceutical companies are able to create their own version of the medicine.

The type and quantity of the active ingredient in the generic product is the same as the branded version, but the inactive ingredients are slightly different. The generic medicine is sold under a different brand name and it may look different (e.g. in colour or shape) to the original.

A **pseudo-generic** product is not a remake of the original; it is an exact replica of the original. It is made by the same company with exactly the same ingredients in the same way. The only difference is the name and packaging.

These medicines are usually marketed by the same manufacturer at the same price as the original. Pharmaceutical companies make pseudo-generic products to combat true generics and to discourage competitor pharmaceutical companies from entering the market for that particular medicine.

Knowledge Byte 5

Hospital Admission/Discharge

A person can only be admitted to a hospital if a physician determines that person requires sophisticated nursing care around the clock, or other specialized professional services or monitoring, or special equipment or facilities that only a hospital can provide, or which, because of the patient's condition, can best be provided in the hospital setting (for example, multiple clinical problems where the patient needs or benefits from having the various diagnostic and treatment modalities all in one place). Furthermore,a person can only be admitted to a hospital if a physician who is authorized by the hospital to do so (not necessarily the physician who made the initial determination), agrees to be responsible for the management of that person's care while in the hospital.

Typical reasons for a hospital admission: planned surgery that requires at least a couple of days monitoring by professionals, especially nurses, during the postoperative period; serious injuries (bad fall, automobile accident); serious medical condition (stroke, heart attack);

risky medications that have to be administered and monitored by skilled professionals.

Hospital admission involves staying at a hospital for at least one night or more.

Staying in the hospital overnight is done because the individual is too sick to stay at home, requires 24-hour nursing care, and/or is receiving medications and undergoing tests and/or surgery that can only be performed in the hospital setting.

Description

An individual may be admitted to the hospital for a positive experience, such as having a baby, or because they are undergoing an elective surgery or procedure, or because they are being admitted through the emergency department. Being admitted through the emergency department is the most stressful of these circumstances because the event is unexpected and may be a major life crisis.

Before the person is taken to their room, admitting procedures are performed. The person's personal data is recorded and entered into the hospital's computer system. This data may include:

- name
- address
- home and work telephone number
- date of birth
- place of employment
- occupation

- emergency contact information, or the names and telephone numbers of those individuals the hospital should contact if the person being admitted needs emergency care or their condition worsens significantly
- insurance coverage
- reason for hospitalization
- allergies to medications or foods
- religious preference, including whether or not one wishes a clergy member to visit

There may be several forms to fill out.

One form may be a detailed medical and medication history. This history will include past hospitalizations and surgeries. Having this information readily available will make the process move faster, and can allow a family member or friend who is accompanying the person to help fill out the forms more easily.

The hospital may ask if there are any advance directives. This refers to forms that have been filled out indicating what medical decisions one wants others to make on their behalf.

One form is called a living will and clearly tells which specific resuscitation efforts the person does or does not want to have performed on them in order to save or extend their life.

Another form may be a durable power to attorney. This is a form stating whom the patient wishes to make medical decisions for them if they themselves are unable to do so, such as if they are in a coma.

Some hospitals have blank forms that the individual can use to make these designations, others may just ask if the forms have been filled out, and if so to add a copy of them into the person's medical record. They are considered legally binding, and an attorney can assist in filling them out.

During the time spent in admitting, a plastic bracelet will be placed on the person's wrist with their name, age, date of birth, room number, and medical record number on it. A separate bracelet is added that lists allergies. Forms are completed and signed, so that the patient is giving full consent to have the hospital personnel take care of them while they are in the hospital during that particular hospital stay. Subsequent hospital stays require new consent forms.

Once all the admitting information has been completed, the next step is usually being taken to one's room. Most people stay in a semi-private room, which means that there are two people in a room. In some circumstances, a person's medical condition may require staying in a private room. If there are private rooms available, and the individual is willing to pay the extra cost (insurance companies generally only cover the cost of a semi-private room), it may be possible to have a private room.

Most hospital rooms are set up so that one bed is closer to the door, and the other is next to a window. There are curtains that can be drawn completely around the bed so that some degree of privacy is possible. Once taken to a room, the nurse taking care of the patient will go over the medical and medication history, and orient the person to the room. This means that they will explain how to adjust bed height, how to use the nurse call button, show where the bathroom is located, and explain how to use the bedside telephone and television. The cost for the telephone and television are not usually covered by insurance.

There is usually a calendar in the room, to help the patient keep track of the date, as it can be disorienting to be in an unfamiliar place, especially over several days or weeks. There may be limitations on using the bathroom, if the person's doctor feels that the patient's condition is such that they should not get out of bed. These kinds of decisions are made with the person's safety and medical condition in mind. If the person is not thinking clearly, perhaps because of some medication they are receiving, the side rails of the bed may be put up, to prevent falling out of bed. The nurse will review the doctor's orders, such as what tests have been scheduled, whether or not they can get out of bed for the bathroom or to walk around the unit, what medications they will be getting, and whether or not there are restrictions on what they can eat. The hospital will supply towels, sheets, and blankets, but some people like to bring something personal with them from home. Because of the risk of infections being transferred from one patient to another, one may prefer to leave things at home. If one does choose to bring in something personal, it should be washed with warm or hot water and soap to make sure that germs are not brought home from the hospital.

Sometimes when people are admitted to the hospital they need extremely close observation that can only be given in specialized care called an intensive care unit . Because of the severity of their condition, visiting hours are more restricted than in the regular rooms. It may be that only one or two people can visit at a time, and only for a few minutes at a time. Once the person's condition improves, they may then be transferred to a room with a less rigid visitation policy. If an individual has a surgical procedure performed, they will spend a few hours in a recovery area. This is to make sure that the person's condition is stable before returning to the regular room. Visiting is limited in the recovery area, and the person may spend most of the time sleeping, as the effects of the surgical anesthesia wear off.

If the person entering the hospital is a child, the parents or guardian will fill out the hospital forms. Most hospitals allow parents and guardians to stay overnight in the hospital with the child, and to be with them 24 hours a day. Many hospitals have special areas for children to play in, and even areas in which they do not have anything done to them which is painful, so they can completely relax.

Preparation

If the hospitalization is prearranged, there are preparations that will make the process go more smoothly. It is helpful to have a list of all medications currently being taken, the dosages, how often they are taken, and the reason for taking them. The list should also include any allergies to food and medications, including a description of the reaction, and when the food or medication was last taken. The list should include over-the-counter (OTC) and prescription medications, vitamins, supplements, and herbal and home remedies.

If the hospital stay involves surgery in which there is the potential for significant blood loss, it may be possible to arrange to have blood drawn and stored so that in the event of a transfusion, the individual receives his or her own blood.

If the hospital stay is an extended one, a list of family and friends, with their telephone numbers, can make it easier to stay in touch with people who can come and visit, or offer support by telephone. It is not a good idea to bring anything of value to the hospital as there are many times when one could be out of the room. However, it may be helpful to have some pocket change available if one needs to make some small purchases at the hospital gift shop, such as a newspaper. If one is going to visit someone in the hospital, change or one dollar bills to use at vending machines may come in handy.

A small bag can be brought into the hospital that contains.

Night clothes (The hospital supplies their own, but some people like to wear familiar clothing; some people use the hospital outfits to decrease the chance of staining their own clothing or bringing germs home from the hospital.)

- a robe
- slippers
- clothes for the return trip home
- reading material for the hospital stay

- hobby materials such as knitting or a book of crossword puzzles
- reading glasses
- personal care items such as comb, brush, and toothbrush (most hospitals supply these items, but many individuals prefer to have their own from home)
- It is best not to bring in any medication from home unless it has been prearranged with the physician and hospital staff prior to hospitalization. This is to prevent an error from occurring by having the person taking one dose from their own medicine and then being given another dose from the hospital pharmacy.

Discharge from hospital

Discharge from the hospital is the point at which the patient leaves the hospital and either returns home or is transferred to another facility such as one for rehabilitation or to a nursing home. Discharge involves the medical instructions that the patient will need to fully recover. Discharge planning is a service that considers the patient's needs after the hospital stay, and may involve several different services such as visiting nursing care, physical therapy, and home blood drawing.

Description

Hospitalization is often a short-term event, so planning for discharge may begin shortly after admission. The physicians, nurses, and case managers involved in a patient's care are part of an assessment team that keeps in mind the patient's pre-admission level of functioning, and whether the patient will be able to return home following the current hospital admission. Information that could affect the discharge plan should be noted in the patient's medical record so that it will be taken into account when discharge is being scheduled. The primary questions include:

- Can this patient return to his or her preadmission situation?
- Has there been a change in the patient's ability to care for him - or herself?
- Is the patient in need of services to be able to care for him - or herself?
- Which services will the patient need?
- Are there mental health needs that must be met?
- Does the patient agree with the discharge plan?

While a person has been in the hospital, physicians other than the primary care physician have been in charge of the patient's care. Good discharge planning involves clear communication between the hospital physician(s) and the primary care physician. This may be done by telephone and/or in writing. The information to be conveyed includes:

- a summary of the hospital stay
- a list of test and surgeries performed, with results
- a list of test results still pending
- a list of tests needed after discharge, such as a repeat chest x ray

- a list of medications the patient is being discharged with, including the dosage and frequency
- a copy of the patient's discharge instructions
- when the patient should see the primary care physician for a follow-up appointment
- The plan for outpatient treatment, such as home intravenous antibiotics or parenteral nutrition to ensure that responsibility for this treatment has been clearly transferred and that the primary care physician accepts the treatment responsibility
- discharge instructions to the patient on activity level, diet, and wound care

Before leaving the hospital, the patient will receive discharge instructions that should include:

- an explanation of the care the patient received in the hospital
- a list of medications the patient will be taking (the dosage, times, and frequency)
- a list of potential side effects of any newly prescribed medications
- a prescription for any newly prescribed medications
- when to see the primary care physician for a follow-up appointment
- home care instructions such as activity level, diet, restrictions on bathing, wound care, as well as when the patient can return to work or school, or resume driving

- signs of infection or worsening condition, such as pain, fever, bleeding, difficulty breathing, or vomiting
- an explanation of any services the patient will now be receiving, such as for a visiting nurse, and to include contact information

The term discharge planning may be used to refer to the service provided to help patients arrange for services such as rehabilitation, physical therapy, occupational therapy, visiting nurses, or nursing home care. This service may be provided by a case manager or by the hospital's social service department. The patient may request this service, or the physician may make the request in the form of a referral to the department. The patient will need to be evaluated to see what services he or she requires, as well as what services he or she qualifies for (such as meals-on-wheels), or what services the patient's insurance will cover.

The patient may be discharged home with a visit from a visiting nurse later the same day to assess the patient's need for these services and to make arrangements for him or her in the home. A person may be discharged home only when certain equipment such as a hospital-style bed and oxygen has been delivered to the home. If a patient feels he or she is being discharged before he or she is ready, the patient can file a complaint with the hospital's ombudsman.

A follow-up from the hospital staff, either physician, nurse, or case manager, should take place within two weeks of discharge to review the results of any tests that were done in the hospital that came in after the patient was discharged, to remind the patient of the follow-up appointment with the physician, to see if the patient has any questions about any new medications that were added in the hospital, and to be sure that no problems arose after discharge that have not been addressed. Such follow-up calls help to ensure a successful recovery.

A patient may experience a complication or an adverse effect as a result of care received in the hospital. The complication may be due to medication that was given, or from a test or surgery performed. In the February 2003 issue of The Annals of Internal Medicine, researchers reported how often these adverse effects arose, and how severe they were. Patients were interviewed by telephone a few weeks after discharge. About 20% had experienced an adverse effect such as a new or worsening symptom, medication-related problems, the need for an unexpected visit to the doctor, or death. Of the 20%, about one third had preventable adverse effects, and another third had problems that would have been less severe if they had received proper medical care. Three percent developed permanent disability.

Tips that can help your discharge from the hospital

Plan for the things you'll need to have ready before you leave the hospital, so that you don't have to rush to do it right before your discharge. This can include things like a hospital bed or wheelchair, bandages, and skin care items. It may also include arranging for help with personal care and household chores.

Ask for written discharge instructions and a summary of your current health status. Bring this information to all of your follow-up medical appointments.

Most hospitals have discharge planners on staff. They can help you find community resources to help you develop your discharge plan. They can also help you understand your medical insurance coverage.

If you're unclear about any part of your hospital discharge instructions, don't hesitate to ask the members of your hospital care team to repeat the information or to explain it more clearly.

Knowledge Byte 6

Rights & Responsibilities of Patients

Overview of Patients' rights in India:

1. Right to information.
2. Right to records and reports
3. Right to Emergency Medical Care
4. Right to informed consent
5. Right to confidentiality, human dignity and privacy.
6. Right to second opinion
7. Right to transparency in rates, and care according to prescribed rates wherever relevant
8. Right to nondiscrimination
9. Right to safety and quality care according to standards
10. Right to choose alternative treatment options if available
11. Right to choose source for obtaining medicines or tests

12. Right to proper referral and transfer, which is free from perverse commercial influences
13. Right to protection for patients involved in clinical trials
14. Right to protection of participants involved in biomedical and health research
15. Right to take discharge of patient, or receive body of deceased from hospital
16. Right to Patient Education
17. Right to be heard and seek redressal

(Source:http://clinicalestablishments.gov.in/WriteReadData/8431.pdf)

Responsibilities of patients and caretakers

Along with promoting their rights, patients and caretakers should follow their responsibilities so that hospitals and doctors can perform their work satisfactorily.

1. Patients should provide all required health related information to their doctor, in response to the doctor's queries without concealing any relevant information, so that diagnosis and treatment can be facilitated.
2. Patients should cooperate with the doctor during examination, diagnostic tests and treatment, and should follow doctor's advice, while keeping in view their right to participate in decision making related to treatment.

3. Patients should follow all instructions regarding appointment time, cooperate with hospital staff and fellow patients, avoid creating disturbance to other patients, and maintain cleanliness in the hospital.
4. Patients should respect the dignity of the doctor and other hospital staff as human beings and as professionals. Whatever the grievance may be, patients/caregivers should not resort to violence in any form and damage or destroy any property of the hospital or the service provider.
5. The Patients should take responsibility for their actions based on choices made regarding treatment options, and in case they refuse treatment.

(Source: http://clinicalestablishments.gov.in/WriteReadData/8431.pdf)

Conclusion

Let's join hands to make India "the country of the Millions of Real-life heroes" by 2025 where there will be zero incident when any operations/surgeries will be delayed due to unawareness of Healthcare Education.

Annexure

Now registered free* for Electronic Health Records service by visiting – MDHL – My Digital Health Locker (https://app.mdhl.in/)

Hospital discharge Checklist

https://hemangpajwani.com/hospital-discharge-checklist/

Road to buy best Health Insurance

https://hemangpajwani.com/
road-to-buy-best-health-insurance/

Making a health insurance claim

https://hemangpajwani.com/
making-a-health-insurance-claim/

Prescriptions abbreviations

https://hemangpajwani.com/prescriptions-abbreviations/

Sources

https://fit.thequint.com/

https://friends2support.org/

https://www.kokilabenhospital.com/

https://www.stmaryskc.com/

http://clinicalestablishments.gov.in/

https://www.thebetterindia.com/

https://www.indiatoday.in/

https://www.notto.gov.in/

https://en.wikipedia.org/

https://blogs.medibuddy.in/

https://www.quora.com/

https://www.cdc.gov/

https://blogs.webmd.com/

https://medlineplus.gov/

https://www.apollopharmacy.in/

https://www.pittsburghhealthcarereport.com/

https://www.drugs.com/

https://healthengine.com.au/

https://www.verywellhealth.com/

https://www.quora.com/

https://www.surgeryencyclopedia.com/

https://www.gethealthystayhealthy.com/

https://www.truenorthitg.com/

https://www.healthit.gov/

Sources

https://www.mayoclinic.org/

https://www.webmd.com/

https://capo.wildapricot.org/

http://www.bccancer.bc.ca/

https://www.moneycontrol.com/

https://mdhl/in

www.ingramcontent.com/pod-product-compliance
Ingram Content Group UK Ltd.
Pitfield, Milton Keynes, MK11 3LW, UK
UKHW021655190726
13853UKWH00001B/282